English
Exercises

CHERRY HILL

STOREY

Storey Books

The mission of Storey Communications is to serve our customers
by publishing practical information that encourages personal
independence in harmony with the environment.

Edited by Deborah Burns and Aimee Poirier
Cover design by Eugenie Delaney
Cover photographs by Richard Klimesh
Text design by Cindy McFarland
Production assistance by Susan Bernier and Jen Jepson
Line drawings designed by Cherry Hill and drawn
   by Peggy Judy

Printed in Canada by Transcontinental Printing
10 9 8 7 6 5 4 3 2 1

Library of Congress Cataloging-in-Publication Data

Hill, Cherry, 1947–
   Advanced English exercises / by Cherry Hill.
      p.   cm. — (Arena pocket guide)
   ISBN 1-58017-043-9 (pbk. : alk. paper)
   1. Horsemanship. 2. Horses — Training. I. Title. II. Series:
Hill, Cherry, 1947–   Arena pocket guide.
SF309.H62 1998
798.2'3—dc21   97-49047
                                                              CIP

Advanced English Exercises

Arena exercises are a cross between gymnastics, meditation, and geometry. They are essential keys for discovering many important principles about training and riding.

Goals

- Fine-tune transitions and changes of direction
- Master lateral work
    Counter-flex
    Shoulder in
    Walk pirouette
    Half pass
    Full canter pirouette
- Improve collection
    Collected trot
    Collected canter
    Volte
- Learn lead changes
    Counter-canter
    Flying change

Remember as you practice that it is the QUALITY of the work that is most important. It is a much greater accomplishment to do simple things well than it is to stumble through advanced maneuvers in poor form and with erratic rhythm. Keep your mind in the middle and a leg on each side.

How Can You Tell If the Work Is Correct?

1. Work regularly with a qualified instructor.

2. Ask a qualified person to stand on the ground, observe your exercises, and report to you what he or she sees.

3. Have someone record your exercises on videotape. Then watch the tape carefully using slow motion and freeze frame.

4. As you ride, watch yourself and your horse in large mirrors on the wall.

5. Without moving your head, glance down at your horse's shoulders, neck, poll, and eye during different maneuvers to determine if he is correct up front.

6. Ultimately, the key is to develop a *feel* for when things are going right and when they are going wrong by utilizing all of the above feedback techniques. Answer the following by feeling, not looking:

* Is there appropriate left to right balance on my seat bones? Can I feel them both?
* Can I feel even contact on both reins?
* Is the front to rear balance acceptable or is the horse heavy on the forehand, croup up, back hollow?
* Is the rhythm regular or does the horse speed up, slow down, or break gait?
* Is my horse relaxed or is his back tense?
* Is he on the bit or above or behind it?
* Am I posting on the correct diagonal?
* Is my horse cantering on the correct lead?
* Can I tell when his inside hind leg is about to land?

What Do You Do When Things Go Wrong?

1. Review each component of an exercise.

2. You may need to return to some very basic exercises to establish forward movement, acceptance of contact, or response to sideways driving aids. Returning to simple circle work will often improve straightness and subsequently improve lateral work and collection.

3. Ride an exercise that the horse does very well, such as the walk-trot-walk transition. Work on purity and form.

4. Perform a simpler version of the exercise. If it is a canter exercise, try it at a walk or trot first.

5. Perform the exercise in the opposite direction. Sometimes, because of an inherent stiffness or crookedness in a horse, you will have difficulty with an exercise to the left but no problems to the right! Capitalize on this by refining your skills and the application of your aids in the "good" direction and then return to the "hard" direction with a renewed sense of what needs to be done. I often find that doing work to the right improves work to the left.

Counter-Flex

- Working trot, sitting.
- Right corner with normal bend.
- Straight 1–2 strides.
- Counter-flex 2–3 strides.
  - While hind legs continue to follow front legs
    and stay on the line of the exercise, the neck and
    head are brought to the left with a left direct
    rein and right supporting rein.
- Straight 1–2 strides.
- Counter-flex 2–3 strides.
- Straight 1–2 strides.
- Right corner with regular bend.
- Straight 1 stride.
- Counter-flex 2–3 strides.
- Straight 1 stride.
- Counter-flex around the corner and for 1 stride
  beyond.
- Straight 4–5 strides.
- Counter-flex 3–4 strides.
- Straight 1 stride.
- Right corner normal bend.

★ The counter-flex can be performed at the walk
  and canter.
★ Vary where and how long you ask for counter-flex.
★ Counter-flex is not a lateral movement. The hind
  legs follow the front legs on their normal track.
★ Sometimes it is necessary to ride the counter-flex
  exercise as a counter-bend because as the horse's
  nose is brought to the left in this counter-flex
  exercise, the hindquarters automatically want to
  move to the right. The rider might have to apply a
  strong right leg behind the girth and is in essence
  bending the horse around his left leg, thus in a
  counter-bend.

The counter-flex teaches a horse to stay up on the outside rein. For example, when tracking left, if a horse overbends to the left and avoids taking contact with the right rein, counter-flex the horse to the right.

Shoulder In

- Trot to the right, immediately after the corner.
- Perform a shoulder in right.
  - Bring horse's forehand in 30–35 degrees maximum so the left shoulder is in front of the right hind leg.
  - Weight right seat bone slightly.
  - Right leg at the girth pushes the horse forward, activates the right hind leg, maintains the position and the subsequent forward and sideways movement of the right hind, creates right bend.
- Left leg behind the girth prevents the left hind from stepping to the left. (Don't depend on the rail or wall to do this for you!)
- Left rein controls tempo and bend in the neck.
- Right rein guides the horse in to the right and maintains the degree of right bend.
- Straighten horse by bringing forehand back to the original track.

- ★ There are three tracks in a shoulder in right:
  1. Left hind
  2. Right hind and left front
  3. Right front
- ★ The right legs cross in front of the left legs with the right hind reaching well forward toward the left front.
- ★ Shoulder in is the cornerstone of training for straightening, collection, and hind leg activity.
- ★ If the inside rein is too strong, the horse will be overbent and will bulge on the outside shoulder making it look like a "neck in" rather than a "shoulder in."
- ★ If the horse tilts his head (when tracking right, the right ear will be lower), it is usually because the

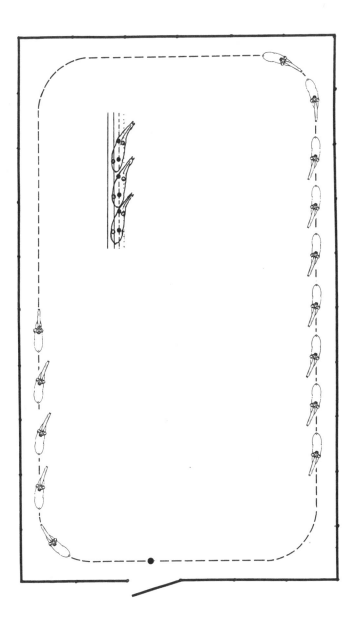

left rein is too strong. Lighten both reins, lift the right rein momentarily, and resume.

★ If the horse gets behind the bit or shortens his stride, return to the straight track and ride actively forward.

Collected Trot

- Ride the working trot, sitting.
- Perform the half halt.
  - Close your lower legs on the horse's sides, and keep your knees down.
  - Tighten your abdominals.
  - Deepen your seat bones.
  - Hold your shoulders back slightly.
  - Squeeze reins with both hands.
  - Let horse's front end come up a bit.
  - Keep driving with your lower legs.
- Repeat this for a few strides (collected trot).
- Resume the working trot.

Description

The collected trot is performed at the same tempo as the working trot but with shorter steps, more marked cadence, more joint flexion, a rounded

back, and well-engaged hindquarters, which result in a naturally (not forced) elevated neck and more vertical flexion in the poll. This is an energetic trot with the balance shifted rearward, allowing free shoulder movement. This trot has the shortest moment of suspension and therefore covers the least ground. The hind feet usually do not reach the imprint of the front feet.

* The best way to *teach* a horse what you want is to show him a very distinct difference between a working trot and a collected trot for a few strides.
* The best way to develop collected gaits is to perform a large number of upward and downward transitions.
* Practice the collected trot on straight lines first. Tight turns and small circles can cause a loss of rhythm and position.

The collected trot is used in second-level dressage.

Collected Canter

- Working canter right lead.
- Canter the right corner.
- Straight 2–3 strides with half halts each stride.
- Collected canter 35-foot circle.
- Keep yourself and your horse very straight in the circle.
- Apply half halts in rhythm with every canter stride, just as the horse comes up in front.
- Ride "in position," but ease with your inside rein so the stride can go forward; otherwise the horse may trot.
- Ride straight 2–3 strides at working canter.
- Half halt.
- Collected canter 35-foot circle.
- Straight 2–3 strides at working canter.
- Half halt.
- Collected canter 35-foot circle.
- Retain collected canter and ride the short end.
- After the second corner of the short end, regular canter straight ahead.

- ★ The collected canter is the only gait in which the horse is ridden in a slightly inward flexion (position in) even on straight lines.
- ★ The collected canter is used in third-level dressage.
- ★ The collected canter develops balance and roundness, improves rhythm, and increases strength and carrying capacity of the inside hind leg.
- ★ The circles test if the horse really stays up on the outside rein.
- ★ Take your time and develop the collected canter gradually.

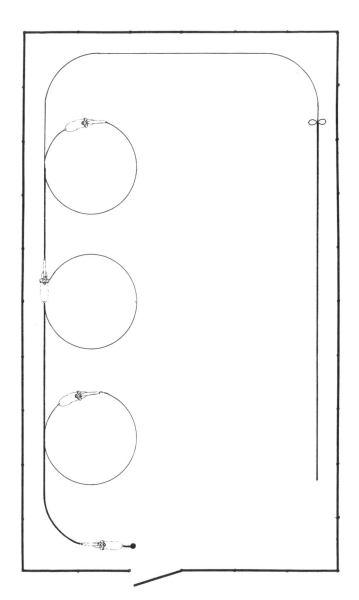

Don't lean in or you could cause your horse's shoulder to drop into the circle and the outside hind to swing out of the circle. If you try to hold the stride length down with the reins, you will likely cause the horse to trot or perform a four-beat canter.

6–Meter Circle: Volte

- Collected trot.
- Ride the corner.
- Ride straight 20 feet.
- Prepare for right volte.
  - Right rein to flex horse vertically at poll and inside to the right.
  - Weight inside heel so horse can balance your weight.
  - Maintain outside rein to prevent overbending.
  - With your right leg, ask for maximum lateral bend while keeping the horse's hind legs following the fronts.
- Ride a small circle (volte) that is 20 feet.
- Ride straight 60 feet or so.
- Right flexion.
- Ride a volte to the right.
- Ride straight.

Only use this exercise in true collected gaits because it requires the most acute lateral bend possible while keeping the horse aligned.

- ★ Develops collection and increases strength of hindquarters.
- ★ Improves Prix St. George dressage.
- ★ For a variation, ride at collected walk or collected canter or ride 2–3 voltes in the same place.
- ★ Don't sacrifice rhythm for the extreme bend required for this very small circle. If you find the horse starts prancing (moving with mincing steps) or getting behind the bit, practice with larger circles and work your way down over a period of weeks.

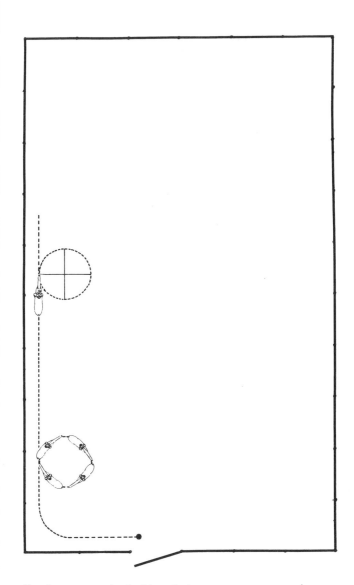

Don't overuse the inside rein in an attempt to make a sharp bend — you will throw your horse off balance, and he will begin falling apart. Never attempt a circle smaller than 20 feet in diameter because a horse cannot bend and stay aligned in a figure smaller than that. His hindquarters would fall out of the circle and his rhythm would become irregular.

Counter-Canter — Shallow Loop

- Collected canter right lead with position right throughout.
- Right corner.
- Up the long side.
- Right corner.
- Short end.
- Right corner.
- Maintain bend (position) to right and counter-canter.
  - Half halt and forward seat to keep horse balanced up front.
  - Weight in right seat bone and deep into right heel.
  - Right rein so horse remains flexed toward the leading foreleg (right).
  - Keep left leg on behind the girth to maintain right canter.
  - Maintain positive contact with supporting (left) rein to balance and direct horse through the turns, to keep horse on the lines of the exercise, to prevent horse from falling out over the left shoulder, to prevent horse from over-flexing to right.
  - Keep your hips parallel to horse's hips.
  - Keep your shoulders parallel to horse's shoulders.
- Return to the rail and maintain right position for a stride or two.
- Straighten.

This exercise helps to:
- ★ Strengthen horse's loins and engage hind legs.
- ★ Prepare the horse for flying change.
- ★ Balance the canter.
- ★ Enhance first-level dressage.

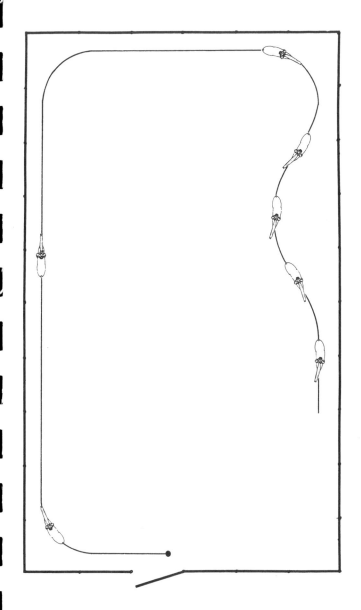

Be sure not to shift your weight or your horse might break gait or perform a flying lead change. Don't get tense or stiff because you will cause the canter to become stilted. Don't leg yield to and from the rail. You must ride your horse "forward" on the curved line.

Walk Pirouette

- Collected walk up the long side.
- At the midpoint, half halt.
- Walk pirouette right.
  - Flex the horse to the right and guide him into the turn with the right rein.
  - Left rein controls degree of right flexion but allows movement for turn to right.
  - Weight right seat bone.
  - Keep upper body straight.
  - Left shoulder forward.
  - Right leg at the girth to keep the turn forward.
  - Left leg slightly behind the girth supporting the hindquarters, preventing the left hind leg from stepping sideways to the left, activating the hindquarters to step forward and sideways to the right in a small half circle.
- Finish turn one horse-width off original track.
- Straighten and walk forward.

If the exercise is performed at a collected trot, the actual pirouette is performed at a collected walk. The horse should not come to a full halt before or after the turn.

Footfall pattern of a walk pirouette to the right is the same as the walk: left hind, left front, right hind, right front. The horse is flexed to the right. The pivot point is the right hind. The right hind moves up and down nearly in the same spot or slightly in front of it with each stride. The left hind walks a tiny half circle around the right hind. The forehand moves in a half circle to the right, with the left front crossing over in front of the right front.

Note the difference between a pivot point and a pivot foot: The leg of a pivot point marks time by lifting up and setting down in rhythm with the four-beat walk. A pivot foot swivels but is locked in place.

A really active outside leg might cause you to weight your outside seat bone instead of your inside seat bone. Then your horse might use his outside hind leg as a pivot point and could step backward with his inside hind leg to keep his balance.

Half Pass

- Collected trot.
- Coming out of the corner half halt.
- Half pass to the right.
  - Look slightly in the direction of travel.
  - Ride shoulder fore or shoulder in for a few strides if necessary to be sure the shoulder is leading. (This is exaggerated on the arena map to make the point.)
  - Weight right seat bone and heel.
  - Right leg at the girth to keep right hind moving actively forward and to maintain the right bend.
  - Left leg behind the girth pushing in rhythm with trot stride. Left rein controls bend, secures neck at the base, and maintains balance and rhythm.
  - The right front leg should take the first sideways steps.
- Straighten by first releasing the shoulder fore aids and then finish straightening.
- Ride straight ahead.

In a half pass to the right, the horse moves forward and sideways to the right around the rider's right leg, the horse flexed and bent to the right. The horse's body is basically parallel to the rail, with the shoulders slightly in advance of the hindquarters.

The half pass:
* Supples the horse evenly on both sides.
* Develops straightness and balance.
* Develops collection and strength of the inside hind leg.

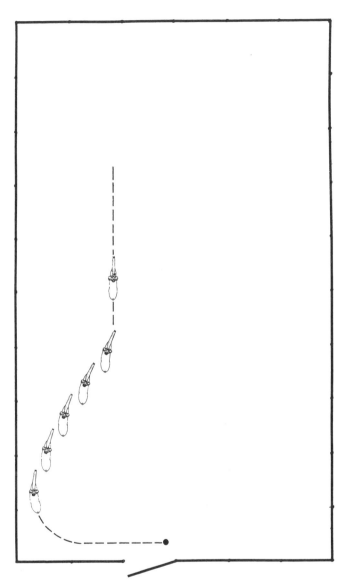

Don't be tempted to weight your left seat bone and heel and try to push the horse over to the right for a half pass right. Take care not to overbend to the right or to let the right hand cross over the mane to the left. If the horse is not bent around your right leg, you are basically performing leg yield — incorrectly!

Full Canter Pirouette

- Collected canter through the corner.
- Half pass to the right, making sure your horse's inside hind (right) is well under his mass.
- Full pirouette.
  - Right leg to maintain forward impulsion.
  - Left leg as for half pirouette.
  - Right rein can be carried a bit higher than the left to cause the horse to flex vertically at the poll (in accordance with the degree of collection of the pirouette) without overbending to the right.
- From pirouette, go into half pass right.
- Straighten.

A full pirouette will take from 6–8 strides of canter.

The full canter pirouette can improve Prix St. George dressage.

The main problems are the hindquarters swinging to the left, a loss of bend to the right, and a loss of the three-beat rhythm. If at any time there is a loss of forward motion in the pirouette, ride forward out of it in an active canter.

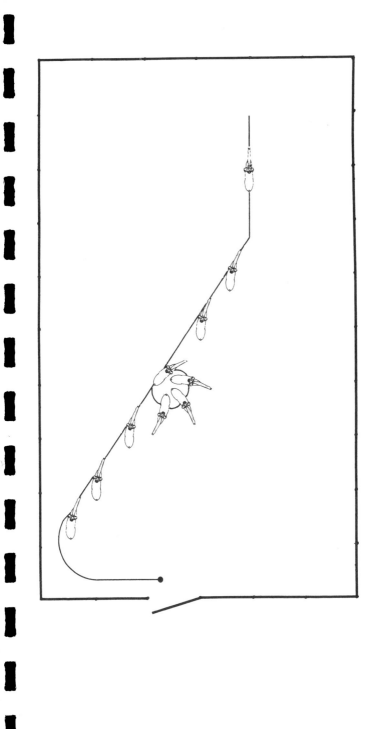

Flying Change

- Canter 65-foot circle on right lead.
- Start across the diagonal with right bend.
- Straighten.
- Half halt (series).
- Before the flying change, prepare by:
  - performing a half halt;
  - changing very slight flexion to left;
  - moving your new outside leg (right) behind the girth but letting it remain passive temporarily;
  - being sure your new outside rein (right) supports the left flexion;
  - hesitating new inside leg (left) in its old position, holding, to help keep the horse's body straight.
- Flying change at moment before suspension, as old leading foreleg (right) is swinging forward to land.
  - Use your new inside leg forward and active to engage new inside hind.
  - Ease new inside rein slightly to allow new leading foreleg to stride out.
  - Weight to inside seat bone without twisting.
  - Outside leg active behind the girth to cause the new outside hind to jump well under and carry the horse's weight.

- ★ A flying change occurs during the moment of suspension between two canter strides. The former inside hind (right) becomes the new outside hind, the first to land and start the new canter, left lead.
- ★ Most horses change more easily from right lead to left lead. If the right lead is more balanced than the left, ask for a left-to-right lead change first.
- ★ Flying changes are easier the more active and forward the canter.
- ★ Flying changes are easier and more correct the straighter the horse is before, during, and after the change.

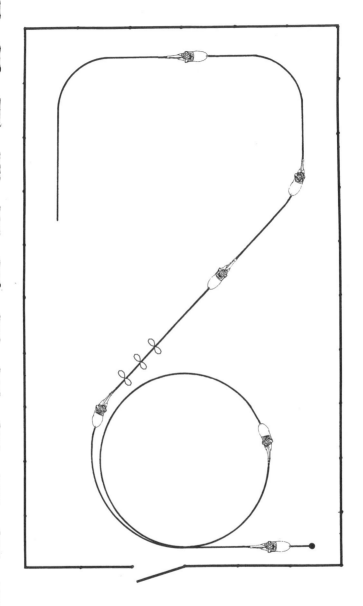

Only attempt a flying change after your horse is soft, supple, and solid and will perform balanced canter departs from a walk. He should also be able to counter-canter and perform precise simple changes with a certain number of walk steps.

Preparing for Your Test

Work regularly with a qualified instructor.

Practice all the exercises in this guide in both directions.

Visualize the test pattern, "ride" it in your mind. Draw the pattern on a piece of paper several times to be sure you know the order of maneuvers.

Practice individual portions of the test with your horse, but don't over-practice the actual pattern or your horse will anticipate. Anticipation leads to rushed work and errors.

Choose your examiner carefully. You may wish to use your regular instructor or another experienced rider, trainer, or instructor. If you ask someone inexperienced to evaluate you, you'll get unproductive results.

Make photocopies of the score sheet. Since you may want to ride the test several times, have extra copies of the score sheet available.

Arrange to have your test videotaped. Later you can compare the examiner's notes with your actual ride.

Rider warm-up. This is accomplished both in and out of the saddle.

Loosen up by giving your horse a vigorous grooming.

Test your suppleness as you squat down to put on your horse's boots. If you are stiff, do some stretches before you mount up.

Once mounted, do a few upper body stretches, arm circles, leg swings, head rolls, ankle rotations, and leg and arm shakes.

Breathe. Throughout your warm-up and your test, be sure you are breathing regularly and properly.

Take air in through your nose, and send it down to fill your abdomen.

Exhale through your mouth to empty lungs and deflate the abdomen.

Especially when you are concentrating and focusing, be sure to breathe in a regular rhythm.

Horse warm-up. Just before the test, warm-up your horse.

Start out at a lazy walk on long reins so your horse can blow and stretch his back and neck and relax.

After a few minutes, sit deep, flex your abdominals, put your lower legs on your horse's sides, and gather up the reins.

For about ten minutes, walk or trot your horse along the arena rail, or make large figures such as 60-foot circles or large serpentines.

Let your horse have a little rest break on a long but not loose rein, as you walk for a minute or two.

Pick your horse back up and practice one or two of the transitions or a lateral or collection exercise from this guide.

Good luck! Ride the test well!

Canter Half Pass — Lead Change

How to Ride the Test

- Canter right lead in a large circle to the right.
- After passing the starting point, leave the circle.
- Ride your horse straight 1–2 strides, parallel with the long side.
- Half pass to the right at the canter.
- Straighten for one stride.
- Flying change to canter.
- Left lead and begin a large circle to the left.

Test Ride Tips

★ Don't weight your left seat bone and heel for a half pass right.

★ Don't overbend the horse's head and neck to the right for the half pass, but be sure his body is bent around your right leg.

★ When a horse is *fully straight* after the half pass, he is prepared and balanced for a flying change.

★ Keep the canter active during the half pass and straightening so the flying change is active and forward.

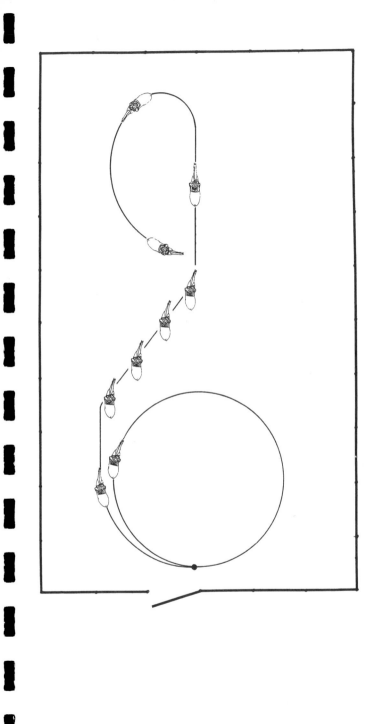

To the Examiner...

You are performing an important role for the rider you are observing. Please study the test pattern carefully and know the exact instructions. Always strive to encourage, not discourage, a rider by your comments. Look for details that can help a rider improve. Try to determine whether it is the rider that needs help or if it is the horse that needs work.

The Numbers. *High scores:* There are so many things that can be improved in a horse or rider. If you give high scores right away, there is less room for improvement. *Low scores:* When you must give a very low score, offer at least one positive comment along with your suggestions for improvement.

Each maneuver, unless otherwise indicated, is scored on a basis of 0–10

   10 = excellent, perfect, took my breath away!
    9 = everything was correct but lacked exquisite smoothness and brilliance
    8 = good job, everything required was performed but overall it lacked finesse
    7 = average job, performed correctly but lacked absolute smoothness, promptness, accuracy, evenness
    6 = minor mistake such as horse bent incorrectly for a few strides or late transition
    5 = one major mistake such as breaking gait for a few strides but then corrected, wrong lead for a few strides but then corrected
    4 = two major mistakes made that were corrected
    3 = three major mistakes made that were corrected
    2 = one major mistake that wasn't corrected
    1 = maneuver did not resemble test requirements
    0 = didn't perform the maneuver

Comments. Be descriptive and creative with your comments — they will help the rider more than numbers because your words will stay in her mind. If you write "poor trot," it doesn't tell much, whereas "a stumble, quick rhythm at beginning of circle, hollow back and short stride" tells the rider much more.

Score Sheet: Advanced English

MOVEMENT	SCORE	COMMENTS
Canter right lead		
Canter large circle		
Leave circle and canter straight 1–2 strides		
Half pass to right at canter (20 points)		
Straighten for one stride		
Flying change to left lead (20 points)		
Begin large circle to left		

TOTAL

80–90	It's past time to move into the dressage competition ring!
70–79	Still an excellent score on very difficult work. Focus more on the areas your examiner identified, then retest in about a week.
60–69	Plan to spend several weeks improving shoulder in, half pass, extended canter, bending exercises.
50–59	Ask for specific help from your instructor to improve balance, precision, control
40–49	Review all of the exercises in Intermediate and Advanced English
0–39	Are you working regularly with an instructor? Is your horse adequately trained?

Other Storey Titles You Will Enjoy

Arena Pocket Guides, by Cherry Hill. Covering both Western and English riding, this six-book series provides illustrated arena exercises and advice for beginners, intermediates, and advanced riders. 32 pages each. Paperback. *Beginning Western Exercises* ISBN 1-58017-045-5, *Intermediate Western Exercises* ISBN 1-58017-046-3, *Advanced Western Exercises* ISBN 1-58017-047-1, *Beginning English Exercises* ISBN 1-58017-044-7, *Intermediate English Exercises* ISBN 1-58017-042-0, *Advanced English Exercises* ISBN 1-58017-043-9.

The Basics of Western Riding, by Charlene Strickland. Covers the Western horse and horse handling, the Western saddle seat, Western tack, becoming a horseman, and trail riding. 160 pages. Paperback. ISBN 1-58017-030-7.

Competing in Western Shows & Events, by Charlene Strickland. Describes Western horse show basics, the show rules and players, showing intermediate riders, showing working horses, timed events, and arena contests. 144 pages. Paperback. ISBN 1-58017-031-5.

From the Center of the Ring, by Cherry Hill. Covers all aspects of equestrian competition, both English and Western. 192 pages. Paperback. ISBN 0-88266-494-8.

Horse Health Care: A Step-by-Step Photographic Guide, by Cherry Hill. Includes more than 300 close-up photographs and exact instructions explaining bandaging, giving shots, examining teeth, deworming, preventive care, and many other horsekeeping skills. 160 pages. Paperback. ISBN 0-88266-955-9.

Horse Handling & Grooming: A Step-by-Step Photographic Guide, by Cherry Hill. Contains hundreds of close-up photographs for feeding, haltering, tying, grooming, braiding, and blanketing. 160 pages. Paperback. ISBN 0-88266-956-7.

Horsekeeping on a Small Acreage, by Cherry Hill. Focuses on the essentials for designing safe and functional facilities on small areas of land. 196 pages. Paperback. ISBN 0-88266-596-0.

Safe Horse, Safe Rider: A Young Rider's Guide to Responsible Horsekeeping, by Jessie Haas. Beginning with understanding the horse and ending with competitions, includes chapters on horse body language, pastures, catching, and grooming. 160 pages. Paperback. ISBN 0-88266-700-9.

These and other Storey books are available at your bookstore, farm store, garden center, or directly from Storey Books, Schoolhouse Road, Pownal, Vermont 05261, or by calling 1-800-441-5700. www.storey.com